While true beauty is the beauty that you hold within, it's perfectly okay to love and embrace your outer beauty.

Beautiful, Wonderful, Marvelous Me!

Written by Letitia Stewart and Sydney E. Stewart
Illustrated by Letitia Stewart

Copyright © 2016 Letitia Stewart
Published in the United States by Letitia Stewart
Printed by CreateSpace

No part of this publication may be reproduced, stored in a retrieval system, or transmitted in any form or by any means, electronic, mechanical, photocopying, recording, or otherwise without written permission of the publisher.

ISBN-13: 978-1530128037
ISBN-10: 153012803X

Dedication

This book is dedicated to all the little girls who struggle with self-confidence. We encourage you to love yourselves, even when it seems like you do not fit into the definition of beauty as perceived by the world around you. Thank you for inspiring this book! Our hope is that you will love and embrace your inner and outer beauty unapologetically!

When I look in the mirror, guess who I see?

The beautiful, wonderful, marvelous me!

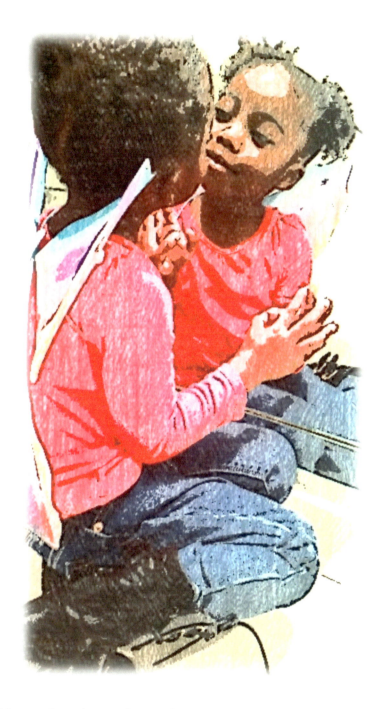

Yes, that's right! I'm as cute as a button!

My skin is golden like the rays of the sun.

Toasty brown, just like a honey bun.

My puffy, black hair looks perfect on me.

My big curly puff sits high like a tree.

And I have lots of style. I love to wear wings.

Fairy wings, that's right, colorful like the spring.

I love wearing pink. Yes, pink is my color.

The pink on my wings, shines bright as the summer!

I'm a very fashionable person you see!

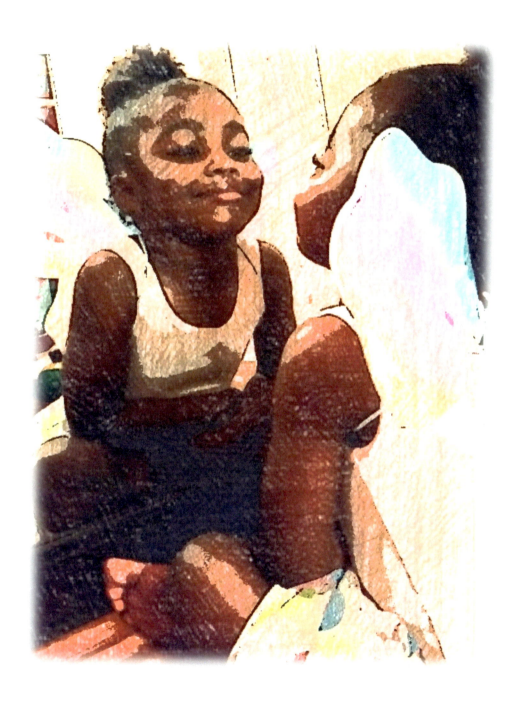

The beautiful, wonderful, marvelous me!

My eyes are big, big, big and round.

They dance when I smile, so sparkling brown.

When I look in the mirror, I never feel down.

Someone like me deserves a crown.

Hmm, a crown would go just well with my wings!

But I'm perfect without one; don't need sparkly things.

I shine by myself – a princess without jewels.

This girl in the mirror is just super cool!

Yes, I'm a pleasure to be around and quite a sight to see.

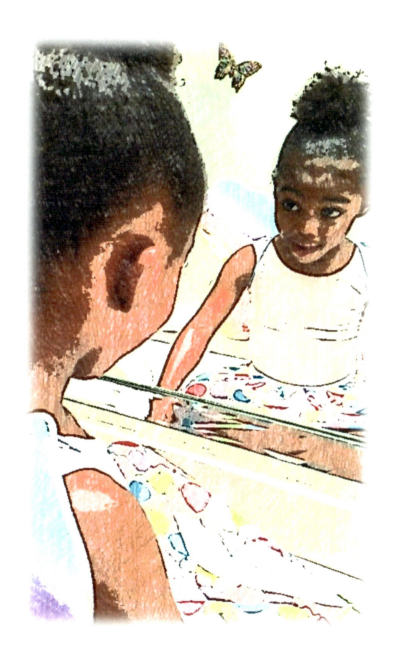

The beautiful, wonderful, marvelous me!

My lips are so full, they round out my smile.

I love to just sit and stare for a while.

My ears are kind of small. My face is really round.

My chin moves up and down, as I smile and I frown.

But my frown isn't real. I'm happy looking at me.

I just love to make faces and love what I see!

Me and the girl in the mirror, we have lots of fun!

We play all by ourselves, without anyone.

The girl in the mirror is me. I'm just fine by myself!

Alone I have a blast, without any help!

Hello me!

I make goofy faces. I act like a goofball!

"You're funny!" I say to the kid on the wall.

I crack myself up! I love to laugh loud.

"Watch your noise!" momma yells. So I sit and I smile.

I wonder how I will be, when I'm grown like my mother.

A bigger version of me, with more beauty uncovered.

Out in the big, big world, with other beautiful faces.

Seeing girls just like me, in big beautiful places.

The world will get to see this reflection of me.

I'm pretty sure they will love what they see,

because I'm a very interesting person to be!

The beautiful, wonderful, marvelous me!

Yes, I'm beautiful I see, but that is just the start.

What makes me more beautiful is my loving heart.

If only this mirror showed my beauty inside.

The love inside my heart does not like to hide.

I love to share smiles. I share hugs and kisses.

I even share my candy so sweet and delicious.

Sharing's a wonderful, marvelous thing to do.

I share my love with others so they won't feel blue.

I'm just a good kid and I love who I see.

The beautiful, wonderful, marvelous me!

My creator was creative when I was created.

Someone as lovely as I am should be celebrated.

I look into the mirror and am truly amazed.

My beauty is a wonderful thing to embrace.

My golden brown skin, my big beautiful eyes,

are no match to the beauty that I hold inside.

My full lips, my big hair, they are all mine.

So I celebrate myself and let my light shine!

Yes, I am quite the work of art. I love who I see!

The beautiful, wonderful, marvelous me!

Did you know that you are beautiful, wonderful, and marvelous too?

Look at yourself! Laugh at yourself!

Yes! You are beautiful, wonderful, and marvelous too!

Embrace yourself! LOVE yourself!

Beautiful, Wonderful, Marvelous Me!

A special THANKS to Victoria Stewart, for contributing your beautiful face and personality to the illustrations in this book! You are truly...

Beautiful, Wonderful, and Marvelous!

About the Authors

Letitia Stewart and Sydney E. Stewart are a mother-daughter team writing children's literature that encourages readers to get to know, love, and appreciate every aspect of themselves. Natives of New Orleans, their books promote reading and learning in a way that is fun, lively, and fulfilling. *Beautiful, Wonderful, Marvelous Me!* is the debut from a series of books to be published promoting self-awareness and self-confidence.

"I was truly inspired to pursue my passion of writing when I saw the same passion in my daughter Sydney's eyes. At a very early age, she exhibited a love for reading and writing, even starting her own book club, the Phenomenal Girls of Excellence. When her teachers advised my husband and I that Sydney had a gift for writing and to nourish it, this has been my ultimate goal. To share this gift with my daughters (thanks for the cool illustrations Victoria!) has been a blessing and an awesome experience!"

Letitia Stewart

"I love writing colorful stories. I have notebooks and notebooks filled with unfinished stories because I am always thinking of new adventures to write about. I have a passion for writing and literature. I write a lot, but my real encouragement is my loving mother. She loves reading my stories and gives lots of constructive criticism (lots and lots!!). However, at 10 years old, I am fulfilling my dream of becoming a writer, thanks to my mom. Writing is my real passion, and I will continue to embrace it."

Sydney E. Stewart

Made in the USA
Columbia, SC
22 November 2024